WHERE WIND MEETS WING

Anthony Frame

SIBLING RIVALRY PRESS
LITTLE ROCK, ARKANSAS

DISTURB/ENRAPTURE

Where Wind Meets Wing
Copyright © 2018 by Anthony Frame

Front cover: *Postcard: mosquito net to be worn as a veil.*
Credit: Wellcome Collection.
Back cover: *A blow fly (Bengalia depressa).* Pen and ink drawing by A.J.E. Terzi, ca. 1919 by Amedeo John Engel Terzi. Credit: Wellcome Collection.
Cover design by Seth Pennington
Interior design by Kathryn Leland & Bryan Borland

All rights reserved. No part of this book may be reproduced or republished without written consent from the publisher, except by reviewers who may quote brief excerpts in connection with a review in a newspaper, magazine, or electronic publication; nor may any part of this book be reproduced, stored in a retrieval system, or transmitted in any form, or by any means be recorded without written consent of the publisher.

Sibling Rivalry Press, LLC
PO Box 26147
Little Rock, AR 72221
info@siblingrivalrypress.com
www.siblingrivalrypress.com

ISBN: 978-1-943977-47-5
First Sibling Rivalry Press Edition, April 2018

This title is housed in the Rare Book and Special Collections Vault of the Library of Congress.

*Death is a Dialogue between
The Spirit and the Dust.*
– Emily Dickinson, "976"

As crude a weapon as the cave man's club, the chemical barrage has been hurled against the fabric of life—a fabric on the one hand delicate and destructible, on the other miraculously tough and resilient, and capable of striking back in unexpected ways.
– Rachel Carson, *Silent Spring*

CONTENTS

- **8** Exterminator
- **10** *Apologia*
- **12** Love Poem with Toxic Tap Water
- **14** Flight
- **16** Pi
- **17** Poem Composed Entirely from the First Lines of Poems by Emily Dickinson
- **19** Swarm
- **21** Dirge with Birds
- **23** Love Poem with Light Pollution
- **25** from *The Gospel of Bullets*
- **27** Adagio for Strings
- **29** Why We Don't Have Children
- **31** How to Hurt a Fly
- **33** After the Funeral
- **35** When Rain isn't Rain
- **36** from *The Gospel of Bullets*, *Part II*
- **38** Equinox
- **40** Poem for My Nieces on the Eve of the Next War
- **42** Cave Poem
- **44** Winter

EXTERMINATOR

Have you seen the boxelder bug?
Its little body, black and curling
along the earth. Its sharp red lines
defining its segments the same way
our veins define our segments.
I've seen it, so close it seemed
I could hear it sing. It seemed
I could almost see it think.
There's an old joke here, about a fly,
a window, and the dying thoughts
of an order of insects that only
knows to feed, to breed, to move
toward the heat of the rising sun.
The beetle flies to the brightness,
then it marches through the grass,
up your aluminum siding, searching
for morning moisture, for silent solitude
among the many. The boxelder bug
doesn't sweat though it looks so,
thanks to the dew that compels it
to crawl up the east side of anything
vertical, anything away from shade.
There's a pun here, about ghosts,
about the soft darkness in hearts,
we who have hearts that aren't
thin slivers surrounded by steel skin.
Watch its eyes, too small to be seen

as they compound me into thousands
of pieces. No, the boxelder bug won't
damage the trees and seeds it lives on
but when you see it, you'll call me,
you'll call it the devil's heart as it
scrambles away from my shadow.
I know I'll kill it and the poison will work
slowly. Still, the dormant Buddhist in me
thinks my mind will be lucky if it returns
as a beetle or a fly. I've seen boxelder bugs
up close. I've seen them burst among
the grass like stars. I watched one die
in the hardened palm of my hand,
the black shell curling in on itself,
the beetle squirming as if it could
consider its next life, the red veins,
the blood pounding our bodies,
our hearts, the eternal eclipse.

APOLOGIA

I'll start at the center, a puff of chemical dust
as I approach the hive, and I know god was here

once. Lately, I've been thinking about hunger,
about bees and pollen, the way a roach will eat

a roach I've poisoned. My hands don't need strength:
residual pesticides, pressurized cans, flush and kill.

Discharge and faith. And I know where to find
the honey bee queen, in the center, deep within

the fractal of the combs. She makes her own light.
Her workers drive their stingers into my protective suit,

a gush of guts as they fly off to die. I want to be
hungry again, wafers and grape juice, an apple

right off the branch. Following fireflies while
walking home from church, dozens of pulses

lighting the night. Look closely and you'll see the bees
look different. And the queen, heavy with eggs

and stored sperm, she won't stop moving,
checking. Is it instinct that makes me touch her,

the way I love to touch the tails of tadpoles?
It's how I learned to find evolution: *lungs, gills,*

spiracles. If I kill this queen, the hive will choose
an egg and feed it royal jelly. Instinct and chemistry,

something to serve. The grand design of the hive.
I want to be human again, afraid and frail, the sun

on my face, sweat on my legs, my soft skin easily
pierced. I want the light of a candle but only remember

the smell of incense. I start here, in the center
of a swarm I started. I crush the queen and I wait.

LOVE POEM WITH TOXIC TAP WATER

It's summer, season of the bloom,
so we drive in search of green,

to see water lilies, marsh mallows,
the frogs and turtles that live

in the algae. Shall we talk about
run-off? Sewage, nitrogen, phosphorus?

Green lawns? We drive outside
the crisis zone to where restaurants

and swimming pools remain open,
the suburbs where microcystin hasn't

taken over. We don't care; we drive
to see the water we can't touch.

We'll touch each other. My wife waits,
watching the lake, its chilled wind

deep in our blood, its tide a lullaby
ringing in our ears. She wants to dive,

our cheeks puffed with oxygen,
our hair learning to fly, our bodies

returning to wild roots. I wait for
official water test results, for rain,

for wind to shift. For weather to do
what we cannot. The stores restock

with water from out-of-state sources
and, for a pair of days, we learn

our limitations, our longing for the air
we steal from her. Lake, lover, landlord,

waiting for us to come back, to breathe,
to dip our fingers deep beneath her skin.

FLIGHT

Follow the horizon, wherever you are
—where lake and sky make love, where birds

both hover and perch. The wind, does it whisper
or whistle? Perhaps it howls—it's up to you.

It depends on perspective, the way the stars
shine in the lake—and if you are swimming,

you are flying, you are trapped between. A beetle
caught in a web, your shell so heavy but without

wings. Away, far away, a nightingale sings,
the sound traveling like a wave, dancing within

the thin clouds. The crows, it's said, are deceptive.
They'll see you—they'll steal your voice and

their squawks will tell the secrets of your sins.
Just because they fly directly, must we hate them

and their reflective feathers? When they speak
with my voice, don't they carry it closer

to the gods I've longed for—the clouds, the moon,
the crows themselves? Look, the horizon

above, unbreakable despite concrete and steel.
Follow, love—follow the angle of the wings.

PI

Let the orbit of his eyes last forever, unpredictable,
despite mixed messages sent from brain to limbs.
Are we more than the fractal of our nerves, a carnival
of fibers, bonded, binding us? We spent a week tracking
a number that refused to end, searching for what we know
we cannot know. Now, I wait to see if skeletons can dance,
to find a tree with branches that match the veins of its leaves.
But for erosion, winter wind, the city's saws. But for
entropy and the wheelchair he'll end up in. Everywhere
is a radius, the suns we drew with sidewalk chalk,
the cells under attack, his wrist as he waves goodbye.
O, infinity, forgive us, you're so close we can almost
touch you. But for decay, but for a spinal tap that uncovers
god's smudged fingerprint. And where is god now
but in the cumulonimbus clouds, towering without center,
waiting to unleash a squall? Unless it chooses not to.
We who believe, he who refuses, let us follow a number
until our eyes sag, until the clouds part and all that's left
to grab is sky. Until the holes in our nerves crash
our dried bodies to the ground. Let us follow as far
as our faith can take us, one number at a time, until
we find a truth. And all the truths hidden deep within.

POEM COMPOSED ENTIRELY FROM THE FIRST LINES OF POEMS BY EMILY DICKINSON

The day undressed herself like rain. It sounded till
it curved, a darting fear, a pomp, a tear—a science,
so the savants say. Behind me dips eternity, a cap
of lead across the sky. Meeting by accident, the sun

and fog contested. Of course I prayed, not knowing
when the dawn will come. Had I not seen the sun
gathered into the earth as if some arctic flower,
could I, then, shut the door? My maker, let me be—

take all away, take all away from me. These are
the nights that beetles love—these are the days when
birds come back. I cannot meet the spring unmoved,
a slash of blue, the long sigh of the frog. Talk not

to me about summer trees—how many flowers fail
in wood? Ah, moon and star, bring me the sunset
in a cup. Blazing in gold and quenching in purple,
a light exists in spring—over and over like a tune.

I'll tell you how the sun rose, lest this be heaven—indeed,
I suppose the time will come—it bloomed and dropped,
a single noon. It tossed and tossed, a little madness
in the spring, trudging to Eden, looking backward.

Take your heaven further on—blossoms will run away.
Perhaps, I asked too large. Perhaps, I robbed the woods.
High from the earth I heard a bird out of sight.
What of that? How dare the robins sing? Split the lark

and you'll find the music. I saw no way—the heavens
were stitched, a clock stopped. This is my letter
to the world: Good morning, midnight—experiment
to me. I shall keep singing. Bind me—I still can sing.

SWARM

A staring honeybee hive, exposed as it tries to find a new home,
in a hole in a tree or above a door, resting now on a branch

as neighborhood children throw stones and try to run as fast
as laughter. It's days like today, Emily, that I miss you most.

Eye of Amherst, phantom mother, here we hear what we want
and nothing more. Not the screams of pulled weeds, not the calm

of bees on a branch. Not the sound of a hive, how it doesn't hum
but shimmers like light, somewhere between a sigh and a shadow.

There's no time to explore the myths of stingers pulled out,
abdomens spilling guts as a bee dies, or the stories of foreign

killer bees waiting in fields and trees. No time no matter how
I want to forget the legends of you wasting away in a white shawl.

What is the truth, Emily? A pair of heliotropes placed in your grave,
bees trying to kiss the pistils despite broken stems. And what to place

in my grave other than a dried hive, the honey finally dripped away,
the eggs that never hatched still glued in their holes? No time to think

about my grave, the tight wood where I'll finally feel dust, where I'll
give back what I've stolen from the earth. Have you heard a hive,

safe in their nest, fanning the eggs, supplying the right warmth?
I have to, Emily, there are more stones than children and both

are slow. Let the bees forgive me for what I'm going to do.
Let them be afraid, enough perhaps to find a crack in my veil.

And if I remove my hood, my mask, if I give them the relief
of the sting, oh Emily, could you dare me to finally breathe?

DIRGE WITH BIRDS
for Rane

Don't say you'll keep me alive with my words.
I wish this ink was boiled hawthorn bark,
black embers dripping off a feather pen.
Who called the birds harbingers? And of what?
One perched on my windowsill last week. Then,
I cut my thumbnail while chopping onions.
The neighbor's girl learned to say *flood* in French.
It won't stop raining. What bird was it,
watching me through the window? A raven,
if I had it my way, Poe's companion,
the unclean one the priests said abandoned
Noah and his dove. But I know the raven
is *Mahakala*, the dharma's protector,
housing and feeding that first infant Lama,
cooing him to sleep as robbers ravaged
the village. And *harbinger* comes from *herbergere*:
to shelter. My yard collects loose pigeons,
so many signs, omens from muted gods,
and were they doves I'd be more hopeful.
Like the ones at church, where I learned to read.
You want me to know the power of words.
You tell me they're roofs, they're chandeliers,
they're feathers. *Words*, you say, you repeat it
two more times. I say never quote Shakespeare
until you've met him in person, as I will,

someday, if the priests are right. If I'm right,
then I've already met him, the shade-crow
who startled me in the night to say
hearts aren't nocturnal. And Whitman, where are you?
Not in the grass, please. Today be a tree
used to create, construct. A house, a shed,
a seed bucket. A frame or casket.
Any shelter to cover this book. Grass
is too soft, restful. Too easily buried
by asphalt, then cracked, patched, repeated.
Too quick to flood, our headstones breaking
the lake's surface like fingers, the new lake
over which the ravens must disappear.
Lake, which comes from *to drain*. When I'm done,
I'll be done with the ground, gladly. Let me drift
with the clouds, sent forth to and fro. I'll return,
passing over your roof, perched above the bed,
holding this grim language, giving it back,
black as ash. Dropping it like a feather.

LOVE POEM WITH LIGHT POLLUTION

You see how hard it is with this light polluting our clouds,
our eyes, our stars, as they reflect billboards and neon bars.
Are we larger now, love, without sky, without constellations,
my bull and your twins faded beneath the fake bright? Take me
as the horizon vanishes, remind me what lives beyond
our bed sheets. Sun-burnt gravity dropping us together,
the ozone hole holding us, our arms and legs as scorched
as the ocean. We drive, searching for a fingernail moon
unfettered by streetlights. There's nothing else to do.
You talk about the flightless kakapo, each rare parrot named,
about the river of five-legged frogs, sterilized by pesticides.
You ask what this means for the honeybees—your garden
of morning glories and amaranth—and I say nothing,
knowing what I've done, the colonies I've collapsed.
Shore me up, love. Let me see beyond the false light,
your wild eyes looking into the vague of space where,
somewhere, the comet ISON flies like our fingers joining,
shooting static sparks. Offer me alternate names for your plants—
Moon in the Dusk, Love Lies Bleeding—and we'll find a star,
if any are out there, to guide us to our lake of blue below black,
the moon our only witness. There, I'll find your legs, we'll let
the moonlight expose our exposed hips, our arms as tight
as our dancing hair. There, we'll fly the only way we know,
down and wet. There, I'm not the kakapo with its frozen feathers.
I can forget my hand forcing the neonicotinoid trigger

into the honeybee hive. We can be small again, two comets,
our orbits defined by our gravity as we rise with the dawn,
the light piercing our bodies as we pierce the surface, gasping,
your fingers clutching my shoulders, binding our breath,
blinding this world, as we swallow the shallow sun.

FROM *THE GOSPEL OF BULLETS*

We who are among you request return, the quick pulse
in our flight no more than a gas station, a secured

bathroom stall, drive-by graffiti. We want to wander,
but our only strength is against gravity and we need

all our strength; we can't come out in peace. Once, we tried
to be water but no one noticed so we turned into a storm,

a gale of hail. We couldn't flow so we learned to ricochet
like the tide; we will always be learning. We were children once,

running through rain and counting clouds, we tested our hands
with chalk and stones. Now, we seek atonement, a word

that means neither *guilty* nor *innocent,* but we receive only
flesh and bone, occasionally Kevlar or a scratched knee,

a skinned rib. If our sorrows can be your sorrows then maybe
we'll learn to be controlled. Stilled. Forgive the mothers

for their wails which could not come out in peace.
God, they've learned, is a smoke-filled chamber,

powder and ash, holes in a car door, or an arm or chest.
Our dreams are of a child dancing, her hair made from

dandelion stems, her breath carrying the quick smell
of clovers. We long for windy fields. Our dreams are filled

with wind. Our dreams are scoured by night, by lust and love
and quiet cells longing. We've waited all our lives for the sunrise.

This is the world we were brought into, blood and thick fluid,
fire and rain. This is our legacy. We measure ourselves in seconds,

we dance but only know two steps. Forgive us. Forgive our lack
of control, our desire to breathe. Our bail is too steep, our bail

is dirt, freshly dug and soft from dew. Forgive our love of
all things wet. We want a hand strong enough to hold us back;

once we start, we cannot come out in peace. Forgive us the holes
we've made, oh lord, so we may forgive you yours.

ADAGIO FOR STRINGS

It's been called the best song to make love to.
Here are pictures of children screaming, mouths

of girls wide enough for us to crawl into. Listen
to the violins, slow, staying slow, ten minutes trying

to blur tranquility and grief. Sand, snow, hook,
pictures frozen on a television screen. I'm standing

on the roofs of my city, I'm standing where wind
meets wing, where it's possible to forget concrete.

The parents inside, do the mothers hold pictures,
do the fathers hold their wives? And how? Like

how does a child pull that trigger? And he was just
a child and so were they. Hidden and hiding, the ones

who survived. Luck looks like a little girl in the arms
of her teacher, luck looks like you and me. You with

your pictures, me with my wife to hold, a television
with violins when live-action audio is impossible.

Here, I'm standing in praise of the surgery that made me
infertile. Snip, snip, hook, the meanness of the world,

the salty corners of an eye. And so we made love.
It's said that Samuel Barber was on summer holiday

and became so moved by the light walking through
the trees, the sublime as the Romantic poets said.

Now, it's the score for dead presidents, falling towers,
first-graders massacred. There where sand can look

like a hook, here where snow seems weightless.
Sometimes, it's frozen: snow, the television,

a child's age. We're all infertile, crawling to couches,
a touch of hands to remind us of warmth, of leaves

one day returning, green buds that slowly open wide
their mouths. Tell me the parents can still make love.

Hidden, hiding, holding pictures. Watching the world
turn or stop, depending on the violins echoing in their heads.

WHY WE DON'T HAVE CHILDREN

We wrap inside each other, all legs and arms
and lips, skin that burns at the touch, her hand
on my chest, my hand beneath the blankets.
Her eyes open and we speak without tongues,
a tribute to the warmth of breath, and outside
the sirens continue to wail. They killed the boy
a few hours from here. It took only two seconds.
Tonight, we wrap inside each other and remember
why we don't have children. Her pink hands
carving sentences into my back, my freckled ears
against her chest, dancing with her heartbeat.
Last week, the cop who stopped me as I walked
to work held his hand ready at his hip, telling me
to take it easy. It's winter but I've yet to lose
my tan and he's always too far to see. He's here
in the bedroom, him and the boy, as we try
to quiet the sirens with our bodies, our eyes
and hair loaded with snow. I could dare a barrel
into a staring match, but it only takes two seconds
to kill a boy. Faster than the sound of a shooting
star. We refuse the bruises of blood, the thrust
of history, the trust inside each splitting cell,
so we wrap ourselves within each other, away
from the constant sirens. We fumble our flesh,

our mouths wide enough to swallow the world.
I trace my tongue along her belly, grateful for
its emptiness. Selfishness is a sin we can
live with. When we leave, we'll leave nothing
behind. The love we make, we'll take with us.

HOW TO HURT A FLY

I wish you'd call so this sunlight can finally make sense,
the automatic lights in my truck cutting off, the traffic
clotting, and, somewhere, you are sleeping.
                                  I still remember
my desk, students fanning the flies that bred beneath the floors.
I told them there was nothing to do, fly control requires access
to the source, a ruptured sewage line, a dead raccoon
rotting in the crawlspace.
                            The sun splits these buildings
as I sit in this traffic and, this morning, the newspaper
described the death of my former student, his body stripped
in an abandoned alley.
                         I know where you are, love.
I was at your side, asleep, five hours ago, but I still need
to hear you say nothing has changed.
                                    Litter and fallen leaves
and what do I remember except that he was lazy,
that he bought his final paper? Sometimes, it's like I'm falling
in this stilled traffic, the way these few clouds seem wasted
without rain, my cigarette rusted between my fingers,
wondering if you're awake yet.
                                 It's possible to pinpoint
the exact time of death based on the insects feeding on the body.
Blowflies are the first to arrive.
                        I remember his nosebleed,

I remember him holding the door for a student with a wheelchair,
I remember him enough to still remember his voice. Some days,
it's like I'm a fly, a quick hum without weight, so say
no amount of punctuation could have saved him.

                                        Say you miss me
too. Say the ruffled blanket isn't enough without my arms,
the books I'll be too tired to talk about when I get home,
the public radio news and few dirty roach jobs
you'll be too lonely to hear.

                                      Did we shred his papers
before the last move?

                    I want to remember your face as it wakes.
I know I've asked so many times but say it again, that light longs
for something to touch. Tell me that when we fall, we'll fall
like rain, our rhythm too quiet to reveal what's left in our wake.

AFTER THE FUNERAL
for my grandmother

What was left and missing   that broken morning
as you walked cloudless   the sky obscene   unmoored

What was left and missing but breath   his final fear

I'll tell you a truth   these words are all wrong
I started to forget him as soon as I felt the weight of his casket

In his Navy portrait he stood taut   like a break waiting

What is left are his eyes   I remember a canopy in his eyes
stars reflected as he watched   patient

He taught me how to stare

Was I in his arms or was it you   I'm sure I fell
and someone jerked me up   what weight   what weight

He told me men want more than sky but I didn't listen

Now that there is nothing   just ash and grass and wood rot
we bear the pall like he taught us   quiet   still

Tell me again   I look just like him

What is left   what remains   the oxygen tank
still sits by the bed   where you taught me to pray

The night he died   this is true   the sky was pink

WHEN RAIN ISN'T RAIN

Sometimes, it's air, sticky but still breathable—it needs no clouds,
as if it comes up from the soil, heavy but too heavy to be held

by gravity. And people walk through it, unaware. The day won't stop
so we ignore it, pretend all oxygen is dry, even though, near the river,

we can see it hovering—we can hold it, we can touch it if we
hold out our hands. Like the girl in the picture on the lamppost,

did you see her? Try and you might taste her purple lollipop.
She used to walk through this neighborhood, here where the police

don't come, where there are cameras on every corner. Sometimes,
rain seems to have a color—even on a day like today, dry as dirt.

It means the swamp is trying to come back, that damp barely hidden
beneath our concrete. It means you can't tell your skin from the wind,

the air from sweat. It means we can ignore anything if we want—
dry rain, damp air, rainbows like halos above the river, children stolen

beneath the sun, within the shadows of cameras. The third girl this month.
Sometimes, the rain is invisible. Sometimes, it's just waiting to be seen.

FROM *THE GOSPEL OF BULLETS, PART II*

We never wanted to be this way, we had hoped for
a breath of air, a chance to stretch our legs, to learn

how to fly, freshness like honeysuckle in the lungs
we weren't made to own. We try but it's always

the same, skipped beats and chairs shattered to the floor.
Forgive us, father, mother, god. We hoped for wind

but can only find veins, bones, tears that never turn
into rivers. And were we fast enough, faster than oceans,

faster than hearts, maybe then you'd take us to waterfalls
instead of churches and schools. The voices you hear

are yours alone; we were made mute, rageless
and without the capacity to sob. It was your fingers

that pierced the leg, that filled the skull with ash
and soot. Forgive us, mother, for hoping, for praying

to finally hear music, a waltz where we can twist
and spin at will. And what do we know about god

except that he loaded us, that his fingernails were chipped
but clean. That he, like us, envied the goldfinch

its freedom. If he sang us to life, he also gave us to you,
but you refused to let us dance. You whispered our names

and we prayed, *No, not like this*. Teach us about fields,
valleys, gardens and pistils, a sky so wide we'll never

touch anything. Show us the stars so we'll no longer long
to mimic them. We've waited so long, bound in boxes,

listening to bird songs, though all we'll ever know is
burst and flash, a hair-thin trigger. Forgive us. We wanted

feathers but you gave us a tail of smoke and ash
too soft to see. Forgive us our love of lakes. Forgive us

our dreams of drowning. We can't stop dreaming.
Forgive us, father, for our weakness before you.

EQUINOX

I'm walking on the still thick ice, catching what cracks
I can find, my wife with a camera in her hands. Later,
those hands will hold me, my eyes will open for her lips.

This is how we worship our city, frozen like these streets,
like the pigeons roosting on top of the building that soon
will be torn down. People are carrying crosses, waiting

for spring. They say start fresh, start from scratch, a nest
raised to the clouds, steel razed to the ground, gloved hands
holding wood too old to splinter. And my hands, brittle dirt,

how did they become so broken? Soon this snow will wash
these streets clean, only potholes left behind, so why can't
the moon do the same to us? Let her learn, let her find

a field where fire waits to bloom, a neighborhood where
god has become an arsonist. Here where river and garden
are both frozen, where we wait for the sun's angle to shift,

just enough to warm the ground, just enough to thaw skin.
Are we wrong? Wanting more than seeds, steel? We've given
our bodies to thorns and stones, to a clouded sky we pray

to one day touch. Lord, now we give you this building,
broken and abandoned. We give you these scarred streetlamps,
this yard overgrown with wildflowers too tall for their roots.

Someone tended these, once, water and fertilizer, rows long
since lost, bodies bare and sunburnt. I take my wife's hand
and we head home where we warm each other with our breath.

This is what happens: hard as glaciers, deep as lakes
carved by a dying ice age, this is how we love here.
And this, maybe, is more. This, maybe, is why.

POEM FOR MY NIECES ON THE EVE OF THE NEXT WAR

When it opened, the boil burst, white infection spreading
from finger to finger. This is how it started, & your father

& I cried while you played in the basement. When we say
we did our best, know that we didn't. When we prayed,

we were silent inside & out. This is the frail world
you were born in, where the structures of our dreams

justify our closed faces. We'll say we did it for you,
& we did, but know also that the urge to resist is strong

but not as strong as the urge to survive, to maintain, to continue
to wake up & work, to tell ourselves there's work still to do.

So we did. We had hoped you'd be old enough to learn
from our relics, our calloused excuses. We had hoped

our fire-white rage could be contained, locked away,
before its sparks reached gunpowder. Now, this white

is dragging us into its blinded self. We could have been
prepared, but instead we spent our lives turning our heads

& our cheeks. Now, faced with our creator, I wish I could tell you we were wise & humble. I wish I could tell you we were beautiful.

We were not.

CAVE POEM

The change has come, slowly, so slowly
we haven't seen. The bees that were once here
      have disappeared. What's left

    are predators in need of prey, stingers
praying for martyrdom. The bees that disappeared
      are taking spring with them.

    Gardens bloom between killing frosts.
Scramble: blankets and leaves. It's time to learn
      a thing or two about stewardship: a boy,

any boy, bent over to catch a frog. Does
he know I can kill a frog just by touching it?
      We need a plague of frogs to replace

the ones we've poisoned. Non-target kills,
we say. Collateral damage. This year the monarchs
      never came. In Mexico, they wait

for word from ancestors, for spirits that bring
answers. But only the clever crows chatter, once
      in your voice, once in mine, but now

mostly in their own. Their voices confer,
they change. The ants, the roaches, the bedbugs:
      the small and subtle shall inherit the earth.

Give them a generation to unlock the key
and, always remember, their generations are short.
We need a plague of locusts to show us

what we've done, what's coming, the hot sun,
the water rising. The Western Black Rhino is gone.
Someone has killed a white buffalo

and her calf. We need a plague that's yet
to be seen. Tornadoes in November, winter storms
we need to name, summer storms

we wish we could forget. Now, the sun feels
closer. Now is the dead season, the deadest month.
What about the crickets and spiders?

Spiders so big they're wolves, crickets so large
you'll curse, you'll scream, *Jerusalem*. What about
the few beasts who manage, somehow,

to survive? When we turn from the sun, when
we run from the disappearing grass, when we return
to caves, what will they make of us?

WINTER

Now we rest, now that the spiders and bees are sleeping,
now that your garden lies beneath fallen leaves and a glaze

of frost, now that all that remains is you and me. This is how
a man wakes up, just as he has since childhood, naked,

damp with sweat after another night of running in his sleep,
but tonight you are there to catch me. This is how a man

is opened, your lips on my thighs, your fingerprints still tattooed
on my shoulders. This is how I learn to let go, all the horrors

in my head as quiet as this neighborhood, this night, and
the man who, years ago, woke me with his scratched hands

and damp beard, the man who stays in my head, in my blood,
how do you keep him from being here with us? I'm a body

of clay waiting for a little water, something to wash away
the dirt deep beneath my skin. It was you I'd been waiting for

all these years, watching as seeds blew from dandelions,
wanting to fly with their feathered fingers. Don't you see,

it was you all along, blowing in my ear, making wind to show me
the turning world, tides to remind me life is motion. That man

took my sleep, replaced it with clouds and streetlights until,
unable to compete, the stars faded beneath the fluorescent glow,

but you turned my eyes into planets orbiting your hips. Now
I have lost my voice, your legs hugging mine, the salt

of your tongue twisting in my mouth, your skin against my skin
my path to salvation, the only sacrament I've ever needed.

Now, molded by your hands, my mind is quiet. Listen, love,
you touched me and I was never the same, these hairs covering

my body hold your scent, they keep your touch safe within
my fragile skin. Sometimes, it takes a twelve hour work day

to drain the nightmares I carry, but what if it only took you
taking off my glasses so I go blind, so I see the sky, my back

bare against the bed so there is nowhere left to go but up,
nowhere but where you are. The world is made mostly of water.

The same is true of you and me, love, so still me, still me
one more time. Sometimes, it only takes your tongue.

ACKNOWLEDGMENTS

My deep thanks to the editors of the following journals where some of these poems originally appeared, often in earlier versions.

The Blue Lyra Review ("When Rain isn't Rain")
The Blueshift Journal ("Apologia")
Boxcar Poetry Review ("Poem Composed Entirely from the First Lines of Poems by Emily Dickinson")
burntdistrict ("Exterminator")
Crab Creek Review ("Pi" and "After the Funeral")
The Dirty Napkin ("Dirge with Birds")
Elke: A Little Journal ("Love Poem with Toxic Tap Water" and "Love Poem with Light Pollution")
The Ellis Review ("Why We Don't Have Children")
Milk Journal ("Winter")
Muzzle Magazine ("How to Hurt a Fly")
Rise Up Review ("Poem for My Nieces on the Eve of the Next War")
The Shallow Ends ("from *The Gospel of Bullets*, Part II")

An early version of "from *The Gospel of Bullets*" was commissioned for The Lament for the Dead Project, a project that sought to use poetry to commemorate the lives of those killed by police officers and police officers killed in the line of duty during the summer of 2015.

"Exterminator" was republished on *Verse Daily*.

I am eternally grateful to The Ohio Arts Council for awarding me Individual Excellence Grants in 2014 and 2016 which provided the necessary funds to work on these poems and on this manuscript.

A number of these poems, lines, images and ideas were generated during my participation in Tupelo Press' 30/30 project. Many thanks to Kirsten Miles, Marie Gauthier and Jeffrey Levine for the space and encouragement. Many thanks also to my fellow Decemberists for setting a bar that I continue to try to reach.

ABOUT THE AUTHOR

Anthony Frame is an exterminator from Toledo, Ohio, where he lives with his wife. He is the author of *A Generation of Insomniacs* and of three chapbooks, most recently *To Gain the Day*. He is the editor/publisher of Glass Poetry Press, which publishes the Glass Chapbook Series and *Glass: A Journal of Poetry*. His poetry has appeared in *Third Coast*, *Harpur Palate*, *Boxcar Poetry Review*, *Muzzle Magazine*, and *Verse Daily,W* among others. He has twice been awarded Individual Excellence Grants from the Ohio Arts Council.

ABOUT THE PRESS

Sibling Rivalry Press is an independent press based in Little Rock, Arkansas. It is a sponsored project of Fractured Atlas, a nonprofit arts service organization. Contributions to support the operations of Sibling Rivalry Press are tax-deductible to the extent permitted by law. To contribute to the publication of more books like this one, please visit our website and click *donate*.

We gratefully acknowledge the following donors, without whom this book would not be possible:

Liz Ahl
Stephanie Anderson
Priscilla Atkins
John Bateman
Sally Bellerose & Cynthia Suopis
Jen Benka
Dustin Brookshire
Sarah Browning
Russell Bunge
Michelle Castleberry
Don Cellini
Philip F. Clark
Risa Denenberg
Alex Gildzen
J. Andrew Goodman
Sara Gregory
Karen Hayes
Wayne B. Johnson & Marcos L. Martínez
Jessica Manack
Alicia Mountain
Rob Jacques
Nahal Suzanne Jamir

Bill La Civita
Mollie Lacy
Anthony Lioi
Catherine Lundoff
Adrian M.
Ed Madden
Open Mouth Reading Series
Red Hen Press
Steven Reigns
Paul Romero
Erik Schuckers
Alana Smoot
Stillhouse Press
KMA Sullivan
Billie Swift
Tony Taylor
Hugh Tipping
Eric Tran
Ursus Americanus Press
Julie Marie Wade
Ray Warman & Dan Kiser
Anonymous (14)

www.ingramcontent.com/pod-product-compliance
Lightning Source LLC
Chambersburg PA
CBHW032103040426
42449CB00007B/1169